CHOCOLATE

simple, sumptuous recipes for every chocolate lover

Marks and Spencer p.l.c.
PO Box 3339 Chester, CH99 9QS

www.marksandspencer.com

Copyright © Exclusive Editions 2003

This edition published in 2005

ISBN: 1-84461-255-4

Printed in China

This edition designed by Shelley Doyle

Photography and text by The Bridgewater Book Company Ltd

Cover Photography by Mark Wood

Cover Home Economist Pamela Gwyther

NOTES FOR THE READER

This book uses both metric and imperial measurements. Follow the same units of measurement throughout;
do not mix metric and imperial.

All spoon measurements are level: teaspoons are assumed to be 5 ml, and tablespoons are assumed to be 15 ml.

Unless otherwise stated, milk is assumed to be full fat and eggs are medium.

Recipes using raw or very lightly cooked eggs should be avoided by infants, the elderly, pregnant women,
convalescents and anyone suffering from an illness.

Optional ingredients, variations or serving suggestions have not been included in the calculations. The times given
are an approximate guide only. Preparation times differ according to the techniques used by different people and
the cooking times may also vary from those given.

CONTENTS

Introduction

Oozing, sticky and sweet, chocolate comes in many guises, from gooey Chocolate Brownies to rich White Chocolate Cake, and delicious Chocolate Chip Muffins. Chocolate has become a luxury item that many people relish, as well as being the illustrious subject of books, films and museums. This gorgeous book will guide you through the most delectable of chocolate recipes and indulge your sweet passions.

Our infatuation with chocolate has developed over many centuries. The botanical name for the cacao tree is Theobroma cacao, or 'food of the gods' and in ages past the bitter chocolate drink of the ancient Incas, Aztecs and Mayas was used in religious as well as social practices. The drink was believed to give a person energy and wisdom, and enhance sexual prowess. Cocoa beans were valued so highly that they were even used as currency!

It was the Spanish explorer Cortez who was first served 'chocolatl', the chocolate drink of the Aztecs, by Emperor Montezuma in 1519. The secret of this bitter drink was kept in Spain by the monks who processed the cocoa, until gradually, the dark and delicious beverage crept across Europe.

And so the obsession with chocolate began in earnest. In France the chocolate drink was the height of fashion at the royal court, and in Britain the first chocolate house appeared in 1657. Then two things happened to change the face of chocolate consumption. In 1847 an English company developed fondant chocolate, and eating chocolate was born. A further step towards the chocolate of today was taken by Daniel Peter of Switzerland in 1876, when he added milk to chocolate. Milk chocolate was here to stay.

Today, chocolate is many things to many people. It is known for providing a burst of energy to the body and has even been taken into space by US astronauts as part of their survival kit! This book will explore the most gooey and gorgeous chocolate recipes imaginable. So take a look, and indulge your senses!

WARM **CHOCOLATE** DISHES, COMFORTING AND DECADENT, ADORN THIS FIRST CHAPTER OF DELIGHTS. MORE TRADITIONAL DISHES SUCH AS BLUEBERRY **CHOCOLATE** PUDDING WITH RUM SYRUP ARE GUARANTEED TO MAKE YOU MELT. AND EXCITING RECIPES SUCH AS **CHOCOLATE** FONDUE, WITH FRESH JUICY FRUIT DIPPED IN DARK SUMPTUOUS **CHOCOLATE**, OFFER THE PERFECT FINALE TO A DINNER PARTY. SPANISH-STYLE HOT **CHOCOLATE** PROVIDES A SMALL CUP OF HEAVEN, ANY TIME OF THE DAY.

HOTCHOCOLATE

PEAR CRÊPES WITH **CHOCOLATE** SAUCE

* **easy**
* **serves 4**
* **15 minutes prep +**
  30 minutes to chill
* **35 minutes cooking**

CRÊPES

125 g/4½ oz plain flour

pinch of salt

3 eggs

250 ml/9 fl oz milk

2 tbsp lemon oil or vegetable oil

FILLING

250 g/9 oz dessert pears

8 cloves

3 tbsp currants

pinch of ground mixed spice

SAUCE

125 g/4½ oz plain chocolate,
   broken into small pieces

2½ tbsp butter

6 tbsp water

To make the crêpes, sift the flour and salt into a bowl. Whisk in the eggs and milk to make a batter. Cover with clingfilm and chill for 30 minutes. Heat a little oil in a frying pan until hot. Add a large spoonful of the batter and cook over a high heat until golden, then turn over and cook briefly on the other side. Cook the other crêpes in the same way, stacking them on a plate. Preheat the oven to 160°C/325°F/Gas Mark 3.

To make the filling, bring a pan of water to the boil. Peel and slice the pears; add to the pan with the cloves and currants. Lower the heat and simmer for 5 minutes. Remove from the heat, drain, and discard the cloves. Leave to cool a little. Oil an ovenproof dish. Stir the mixed spice into the fruit; divide between the crêpes. Fold the crêpes into triangles. Arrange in the dish and bake for 15 minutes. To make the sauce, melt the chocolate and butter with the water in a small pan, stirring. Serve the crêpes with the sauce.

CHOCOLATE FONDUE

* **very easy**

* **serves 4**

* **15-20 minutes prep**

* **10 minutes cooking**

4 tbsp caster sugar

4 tbsp water

250 g/9 oz dark chocolate,
   broken into small pieces

225 ml/8 fl oz double cream

2½ tbsp rum

TO SERVE

cake, such as Hazelnut Squares,
   cut into bite-sized pieces

small whole strawberries, hulled

cherries, stoned

kiwi fruit or pineapple, cut into
   bite-sized pieces

Heat the sugar and water in a small saucepan over a low heat, stirring, until the sugar has dissolved. Remove from the heat and leave to cool a little.

Heat the chocolate and cream in a separate small saucepan over a low heat, stirring, until the chocolate has melted. Remove the pan from the heat and stir in the rum. Stir the chocolate mixture into the sugar syrup.

To serve, reheat the mixture in a fondue pot. Alternatively, reheat in a saucepan, then transfer to a flameproof dish and keep warm, over a small burner if you have one. Serve with pieces of cake and a selection of fruit for your guests to spear on fondue or table forks and dip into the warm mixture.

BLUEBERRY **CHOCOLATE** PUDDING WITH RUM SYRUP

* **easy**
* **serves 4**
* **20 minutes prep**
* **1 hour cooking**

120 g/4¼ oz butter, softened,
   plus extra for greasing
120 g/4¼ oz soft brown sugar
2 eggs
75 g/2¾ oz plain flour
½ tsp baking powder
2 tbsp unsweetened cocoa powder
150 g/5½ oz blueberries

RUM SYRUP

120 g/4¼ oz dark chocolate, chopped
2 tbsp maple syrup
1 tbsp unsalted butter
1 tbsp rum

whole blueberries, to decorate

Grease a large pudding basin. Heat water to a depth of 7.5–10 cm/3–4 inches in a large saucepan over a low heat until simmering.

Put the butter, sugar, eggs, flour, baking powder and cocoa powder into a large bowl and beat together until thoroughly mixed. Stir in the blueberries. Spoon the mixture into the prepared basin and cover tightly with two layers of foil. Carefully place the basin in the saucepan of simmering water, ensuring that the water level is comfortably lower than the basin's rim. Steam the pudding for 1 hour, topping up the water when necessary.

About 5 minutes before the end of the cooking time, heat the ingredients for the rum syrup in a small saucepan over a low heat, stirring, until smooth and melted. Remove the pudding from the heat, discard the foil and run a knife around the edge to loosen the pudding. Turn out on to a serving dish, pour over the syrup and decorate with blueberries. Serve immediately.

CHOCOLATE FRUIT PANCAKES WITH LIME BUTTER

✳ **easy**

✳ **serves 4**

✳ **20 minutes prep +**
   30 minutes to stand/chill

✳ **15 minutes cooking**

100 g/3½ oz plain flour

2 tbsp unsweetened cocoa powder

1 egg, beaten

300 ml/10 fl oz milk

1 apple, peeled, chopped and
   brushed with lime juice

1½ tbsp soft brown sugar

2 large bananas, thinly sliced

115 g/4 oz grated dark chocolate,
   melted

sunflower oil, for frying

LIME BUTTER

150 g/5½ oz butter, softened

1 tbsp finely grated lime rind

1 tbsp lime juice

Sift the flour and cocoa powder into a bowl, make a well in the centre and add the beaten egg. Gradually beat in the flour mixture from the sides, then slowly beat in the milk until smooth. Cover with clingfilm and leave to stand for 30 minutes.

Arrange the apple on a foil-covered grill rack. Sprinkle with a little sugar, then cook under a preheated medium grill for 3 minutes. Turn, sprinkle with the remaining sugar and cook for 2 minutes. Transfer to a bowl, add the bananas and mix well. Put the butter, lime rind and juice into a separate bowl, mix well and chill.

Heat a little oil in a frying pan over a high heat. Beat the batter and pour 4 tablespoonfuls into the pan to make a layer. Cook until firm underneath, flip over and cook the other side. Remove and keep warm. Repeat with the remaining batter. Divide the filling between the pancakes, drizzle the melted chocolate over the filling, roll up and serve with the lime butter.

SPANISH-STYLE HOT CHOCOLATE

∗ **extremely easy**

∗ **serves 4**

∗ **3-4 minutes prep**

∗ **5 minutes cooking**

850 ml/1½ pints milk

200 g/7 oz dark chocolate, broken into
   small pieces

2 tsp sugar

1 tsp mixed spice, to decorate

fried bread, crusts removed and
   cut into triangles, to serve

Put the milk, chocolate and sugar into a saucepan over a medium heat and whisk until melted and gently simmering.

Remove from the heat and pour into heatproof glasses. Sprinkle over the mixed spice and serve with fried bread triangles.

THERE IS NOTHING ON EARTH QUITE LIKE THE RICH SMELL OF BAKING YOUR FAVOURITE **CHOCOLATE** RECIPE. **CHOCOLATE** CHIP MUFFINS ARE A DELICIOUS HOMELY TREAT FOR A MID-MORNING BREAK, OR AN AFTERNOON SNACK. THE ELEGANT WHITE **CHOCOLATE** CAKE AND STUNNING BAKED PEARS WITH **CHOCOLATE** CUSTARD ARE SURE TO CAUSE A STIR AT ANY TABLE. THIS SECTION IS PERFECT FOR TRADITIONAL EVERYDAY BAKING, OR FOR A SPECIAL OCCASION.

BAKEDCHOCOLATE

CHOCOLATE CHIP COOKIES

✳ **very easy**

✳ **serves 4**

✳ **15 minutes prep +**
   1-2 hours to cool

✳ **12-15 minutes cooking**

125 g/4½ oz butter, softened,
  plus extra for greasing
125 g/4½ oz dark muscovado sugar
1 egg, beaten
190 g/6½ oz self-raising flour
2 tbsp unsweetened cocoa powder
1 tsp almond extract
120 g/4¼ oz dark chocolate chips
55 g/2 oz shelled mixed nuts, chopped

Preheat the oven to 190°C/375°F/Gas Mark 5. Grease two large baking trays.

Put the butter and sugar into a large bowl and cream until fluffy. Gradually beat in the egg. Sift the flour and cocoa powder into a separate bowl, then fold into the egg mixture with the almond extract. Stir in the chocolate chips and nuts. Drop rounded dessertspoonfuls of the mixture on to the prepared baking trays, leaving plenty of space between them to allow them to spread during cooking.

Bake in the oven for 12–15 minutes, or until golden. Remove from the oven, transfer to wire racks and leave to cool completely. Store in an airtight tin until ready to serve.

CHOCOLATE BROWNIES

✳ **very easy**

✳ **serves 4**

✳ **20 minutes prep +**

1-2 hours to cool/set

✳ **35-40 minutes cooking**

225 g/8 oz butter, diced,
   plus extra for greasing
150 g/5½ oz dark chocolate, chopped
225 g/8 oz self-raising flour
125 g/4½ oz dark muscovado sugar
4 eggs, beaten
60 g/2¼ oz blanched hazelnuts,
   chopped
60 g/2¼ oz sultanas
100 g/3½ oz dark chocolate chips
115 g/4 oz white chocolate, melted,
   to decorate

Preheat the oven to 180°C/350°F/Gas Mark 4. Grease and line a 28 x 18-cm/11 x 7-inch rectangular cake tin.

Put the butter and dark chocolate pieces into a heatproof bowl and set over a saucepan of simmering water until melted. Remove from the heat. Sift the flour into a large bowl, add the sugar and mix well. Stir the eggs into the chocolate mixture, then beat into the flour mixture. Add the nuts, sultanas and chocolate chips and mix well. Spoon evenly into the cake tin and level the surface.

Bake in the oven for 30 minutes, or until firm. To check whether the cake is cooked through, insert a skewer into the centre – it should come out clean. If not, return the cake to the oven for a few minutes. Remove from the oven and leave to cool for 15 minutes. Turn out on to a wire rack to cool completely. To decorate, drizzle the melted white chocolate in fine lines over the cake, then cut into bars. Leave to set before serving.

CHOCOLATE CHIP MUFFINS

✳ **very easy**

✳ **serves 12**

✳ **15 minutes prep +**
1 hour to cool

✳ **25-30 minutes cooking**

100 g/3½ oz butter, softened
125 g/4½ oz caster sugar
100 g/3½ oz dark muscovado sugar
2 eggs
150 ml/5 fl oz soured cream
5 tbsp milk
250 g/9 oz plain flour
1 tsp bicarbonate of soda
2 tbsp unsweetened cocoa powder
190 g/6½ oz dark chocolate chips

Preheat the oven to 190°C/375°F/Gas Mark 5. Line a 12-ring muffin tin with paper cases.

Put the butter, caster sugar and dark muscovado sugar into a bowl and beat well. Beat in the eggs, cream and milk until thoroughly mixed. Sift the flour, bicarbonate of soda and cocoa powder into a separate bowl and stir into the mixture. Add the chocolate chips and mix well. Spoon the mixture into the paper cases. Bake in the oven for 25–30 minutes.

Remove from the oven and leave to cool for 10 minutes. Turn out on to a wire rack and leave to cool completely. Store in an airtight container until required.

WHITE CHOCOLATE CAKE

* **easy**
* **serves 4-6**
* **30 minutes prep + 9$\frac{1}{2}$-10$\frac{1}{2}$ hours to cool/chill**
* **30 minutes cooking**

CAKE

butter, for greasing
4 eggs
125 g/4½ oz caster sugar
125 g/4½ oz plain flour, sifted
pinch of salt
300 ml/10 fl oz double cream
150 g/5½ oz white chocolate, chopped

CHOCOLATE LEAVES

75 g/2¾ oz dark or white chocolate,
  melted
handful of rose leaves, or other small
  edible leaves with well-defined veins,
  washed and dried

To make the leaves, brush the melted chocolate over the bottom of the leaves. Arrange, coated sides up, on a baking sheet lined with baking paper. Chill until set, then peel away the leaves.

Preheat the oven to 180°C/350°F/Gas Mark 4. Grease and line a 20-cm/8-inch round cake tin. Put the eggs and sugar into a heatproof bowl and set over a saucepan of simmering water. Whisk until thick, remove from the heat and whisk until cool. Fold in the flour and salt. Pour into the tin and bake for 20 minutes, then cool for 10 minutes. Turn out, discard the paper and leave to cool.

Put the cream into a saucepan over a low heat and bring to the boil, stirring. Add the chocolate and stir until melted. Pour into a bowl, cover with clingfilm and chill overnight.

Cut the cake horizontally in half. Whisk the cream until thick, spread one-third over one half of the cake and top with the other, then coat with the remaining cream. Chill for 1–2 hours, decorate and serve.

RICH **CHOCOLATE** ROULADE

* **easy**

* **serves 4-6**

* **35 minutes prep +**
  4-5 hours to cool/chill

* **20-25 minutes cooking**

CAKE

butter, for greasing

125 g/4½ oz dark chocolate, chopped

50 g/1¾ oz Continental plain
chocolate, chopped

3 tbsp warm water

2 tbsp coffee-flavoured liqueur,
such as Kahlúa (optional)

5 eggs, separated

175 g/6 oz caster sugar

FILLING

450 ml/16 fl oz double cream

40 g/1½ oz icing sugar, sifted,
plus extra for dusting

20 g/¾ oz unsweetened cocoa powder

2 tsp espresso coffee powder,
dissolved in 1 tbsp boiling water

halved strawberries, to decorate

Preheat the oven to 180°C/350°F/Gas Mark 4. Grease and line a 35 x 25-cm/14 x 10-inch Swiss roll tin.

Put the chocolate into a heatproof bowl and set over a saucepan of hot water, stirring occasionally, until melted. Stir in the water and liqueur, if using. Whisk the egg yolks and caster sugar in a bowl until pale. Beat the chocolate into the yolks. Whisk the egg whites in a bowl until stiff, then fold into the chocolate. Pour into the tin and bake for 15 minutes. Remove, cover with greaseproof paper and leave to cool for 3–4 hours. Meanwhile, whisk the filling ingredients together in a bowl until thick. Cover with clingfilm and chill.

Turn the cake out on to greaseproof paper dusted with icing sugar. Discard the lining paper. Reserve 4 tablespoons of the filling, then spread the rest over the roulade, leaving a 2.5-cm/1-inch border. Starting from a short side, roll up the cake. Discard the paper. Pipe the remaining filling on top, decorate with strawberries and serve.

CHOCOLATE APPLE LATTICE TART

* **easy**

* **serves 4-6**

* **25 minutes prep +**
  1-1¼ hours to cool/chill

* **40-45 minutes cooking**

PASTRY

175 g/6 oz plain flour, plus extra
  for dusting

2 tbsp unsweetened cocoa powder

3 tbsp caster sugar

100 g/3½ oz unsalted butter, diced,
  plus extra for greasing

1–2 egg yolks, beaten

FILLING

125 ml/4 fl oz double cream

2 eggs, beaten

1 tsp ground cinnamon

120 g/4¼ oz dark chocolate, grated

4 apples, peeled, sliced and brushed
  with lemon juice

3 tbsp brown sugar

whipped cream, to serve

To make the pastry, sift the flour and cocoa into a bowl. Add the sugar, rub in the butter and mix well. Stir in enough egg yolk to make a dough. Form into a ball, wrap in foil and chill for 45 minutes.

Preheat the oven to 180°C/350°F/Gas Mark 4. Grease a 25-cm/10-inch loose-bottomed flan tin. Roll out the dough on a lightly floured work surface and use three-quarters of it to line the tin.

Beat together the cream, eggs (reserving a little for glazing), cinnamon and chocolate in a bowl. Stir in the apples. Spoon into the pastry case, then sprinkle over the brown sugar. Roll out the remaining dough and cut into long, thin strips, then arrange over the tart to form a lattice pattern. Brush the pastry with the reserved egg yolk, then bake in the oven for 40–45 minutes.

Remove from the oven and leave to cool to room temperature. Serve with whipped cream.

CHOCOLATE CLAFOUTIS

✳ **very easy**

✳ **serves 4-6**

✳ **15 minutes prep**

✳ **30-35 minutes cooking**

butter, for greasing

250 g/9 oz cherries, stoned and halved

250 g/9 oz nectarines, stoned and sliced
(any juices reserved)

85 g/3 oz light brown sugar

115 g/4 oz plain flour

1 tbsp unsweetened cocoa powder

3 eggs, lightly beaten

300 ml/10 fl oz milk

2 tbsp icing sugar, for dusting

clotted or double cream, to serve

Preheat the oven to 190°C/375°F/Gas Mark 5. Grease a 25-cm/10-inch ovenproof flan dish.

Arrange the cherries, nectarines and reserved juices in the bottom of the prepared dish, then sprinkle over 2 tablespoons of the brown sugar.

Sift the flour and cocoa powder into a large bowl, then stir in the remaining brown sugar. Make a well in the centre and add the beaten eggs. Gradually beat in the flour mixture from the sides, then gradually beat in the milk until smooth. If necessary, push the mixture through a sieve to get a smoother batter, or process in a food processor or blender. Pour the batter over the fruit in the dish.

Bake in the oven for 30–35 minutes, or until puffed up and golden. Remove from the oven, dust with icing sugar and serve warm with cream.

BAKED PEARS WITH **CHOCOLATE** CUSTARD

* *very easy*
* *serves 4*
* *15 minutes prep*
* *30 minutes cooking*

4 ripe pears
1 tbsp lime juice
2 tbsp red wine
55 g/2 oz butter
4 tbsp light brown sugar
1 tsp mixed spice

CHOCOLATE CUSTARD
1 heaped tbsp custard powder
1 tbsp cornflour
1 tbsp unsweetened cocoa powder
1 tbsp light brown sugar
250 ml/9 fl oz milk
350 ml/12 fl oz single cream
2 tbsp grated dark chocolate

thin strips of lime zest, to decorate

Preheat the oven to 200°C/400°F/Gas Mark 6. Peel and core the pears, leaving them whole, then brush with lime juice. Put the pears into a small, non-stick baking tin, then pour over the wine.

Heat the butter, sugar and mixed spice in a small saucepan over a low heat, stirring, until melted. Pour the mixture over the pears. Bake in the oven, basting occasionally, for 25 minutes, or until golden and cooked through.

About 5 minutes before the end of the cooking time, heat the custard powder, cornflour, cocoa powder, sugar and milk in a saucepan over a low heat, stirring, until thickened and almost boiling. Remove from the heat, add the cream and grated chocolate and stir until melted.

Divide the custard between serving dishes. Remove the pears from the oven and put a pear in the centre of each pool of custard. Decorate with strips of lime zest and serve.

CLASSIC CHILLED DESSERTS WHISPER SOPHISTICATION FOR A HOT SUMMER'S DAY. DEEP **CHOCOLATE** CHEESECAKE LOOKS STUNNING AND TASTES EVEN BETTER, WHILE A SIMPLE YET POPULAR **CHOCOLATE** MILK SHAKE PROVIDES A TOUCH OF FUN AT THE END OF A MEAL. EXPLORE YOUR SENSES WITH WHITE **CHOCOLATE** TIRAMISÙ OR TEMPTING WHITE AND DARK **CHOCOLATE** ICE CREAM.

COOLCHOCOLATE

DEEP CHOCOLATE CHEESECAKE

* **very easy**

* **serves 4-6**

* **15-25 minutes prep +**
  4 hours to chill

* **0 minutes cooking**

BASE

4 tbsp butter, melted, plus extra
   for greasing
115 g/4 oz digestive biscuits,
   finely crushed
2 tsp unsweetened cocoa powder

CHOCOLATE LAYER

800 g/1 lb 12 oz mascarpone cheese
200 g/7 oz icing sugar, sifted
juice of ½ orange
finely grated rind of 1 orange
175 g/6 oz dark chocolate, melted
2 tbsp brandy

TO DECORATE

Chocolate Leaves
halved kumquats

Grease a 20-cm/8-inch loose-bottomed cake tin.

To make the base, put the crushed biscuits, cocoa powder and melted butter into a large bowl and mix well. Press the biscuit mixture evenly over the base of the prepared tin.

Put the mascarpone and sugar into a bowl and stir in the orange juice and rind. Add the melted chocolate and brandy, and mix together until thoroughly combined. Spread the chocolate mixture evenly over the biscuit layer. Cover with clingfilm and chill for at least 4 hours.

Remove the cheesecake from the refrigerator, turn out on to a serving platter and decorate with Chocolate Leaves (see page 27) and kumquat halves. Serve immediately.

WHITE **CHOCOLATE** TIRAMISÙ

✻ **extremely easy**

✻ **serves 4**

✻ **15 minutes prep +**
  2 hours to chill

✻ **0 minutes cooking**

16 Italian sponge fingers

250 ml/9 fl oz strong black coffee,
  cooled to room temperature

4 tbsp almond-flavoured liqueur,
  such as Amaretto

250 g/9 oz mascarpone cheese

300 ml/10 fl oz double cream

3 tbsp caster sugar

125 g/4½ oz white chocolate, grated

4 tbsp flaked almonds, toasted,
  to decorate

Break half the sponge fingers and divide equally between 4 serving glasses. Mix together the coffee and liqueur in a jug, then pour half over the sponge fingers in the glasses.

Beat together the mascarpone, cream, sugar and 50 g/1¾ oz of the chocolate in a bowl. Spread half the mixture over the coffee-soaked sponge fingers, then arrange the remaining sponge fingers on top. Pour over the remaining coffee, then spread over the remaining cream mixture. Sprinkle with the remaining chocolate.

Cover with clingfilm and chill for at least 2 hours, or until required. Sprinkle over the flaked almonds before serving.

BLUEBERRY **CHOCOLATE** SORBET

* **very easy**

* **serves 4**

* **15 minutes prep +**
  1-3½ hours to cool/freeze

* **5 minutes cooking**

500 ml/18 fl oz water
200 g/7 oz caster sugar
4 tbsp unsweetened cocoa powder
125 g/4½ oz frozen blueberries
1 tbsp blueberry conserve

TO DECORATE
Chocolate Leaves
whole blueberries

Heat the water and sugar in a saucepan over a low heat, stirring, until the sugar has dissolved. Bring to the boil, then continue to boil, without stirring, for 2 minutes. Remove from the heat and pour the mixture into a heatproof, non-metallic bowl. Stir in the cocoa powder and leave to cool to room temperature.

Transfer to a food processor, add the frozen blueberries and blueberry conserve and process until smooth.

Transfer to a freezerproof container and freeze for 1 hour. Remove from the freezer, transfer to a bowl and whisk to break up the ice crystals. Return to the container and freeze for 30 minutes. Repeat twice more, freezing for 30 minutes and whisking each time. Alternatively, transfer the mixture to an ice-cream machine and process for 15 minutes.

Scoop into serving bowls, decorate with Chocolate Leaves (see page 27) and blueberries and serve.

WHITE & DARK CHOCOLATE ICE CREAM

✳ **very easy**

✳ **serves 4**

✳ **15 minutes prep +
2-4½ hours to cool/chill/
freeze**

✳ **5 minutes cooking**

6 egg yolks
100 g/3½ oz caster sugar
350 ml/12 fl oz milk
175 ml/6 fl oz double cream
100 g/3½ oz dark chocolate,
  chopped
75 g/2¾ oz white chocolate,
  grated or finely chopped

fresh mint leaves, to decorate

Put the egg yolks and sugar into a large, heatproof bowl and beat until fluffy. Heat the milk, cream and dark chocolate in a saucepan over a low heat, stirring, until melted and almost boiling. Remove from the heat and whisk into the egg mixture. Return to the pan and cook, stirring, over a low heat until thick. Do not let it simmer. Transfer to a heatproof bowl and leave to cool. Cover the bowl with clingfilm and chill for 1½ hours. Remove from the refrigerator and stir in the white chocolate.

Transfer to a freezerproof container and freeze for 1 hour. Remove from the freezer, transfer to a bowl and whisk to break up the ice crystals. Return to the container and freeze for 30 minutes. Repeat twice more, freezing for 30 minutes and whisking each time. Alternatively, transfer the mixture to an ice-cream machine and process for 15 minutes.

Scoop into serving bowls, decorate with mint leaves and serve.

CHOCOLATE MILK SHAKE

* **extremely easy**

* **serves 4**

* **10 minutes prep**

* **0 minutes cooking**

300 ml/10 fl oz milk

2 tbsp chocolate syrup

2 tbsp coffee syrup

800 g/1 lb 12 oz chocolate ice cream

TO DECORATE

150 ml/5 fl oz double cream, whipped

unsweetened cocoa powder,

  for sprinkling

Pour the milk, chocolate syrup and coffee syrup into a food processor or blender and gently process until blended. Add the ice cream and process to a smooth consistency.

Pour into glasses.

To decorate, spoon the cream into a piping bag with a large, star-shaped nozzle. Pipe generous amounts of cream on top of the milk shakes. Sprinkle over the cocoa powder and serve with straws.

INDEX